THE ZODIAC PARADE

A Celestial Journey Through The Stars

Written by Ashley Johnson

Illustrated by Indra Audipriatna

Books & Things Publishing, LLC
4410 Brookfield Corporate Dr. #220149
Chantilly, VA 20153

THE ZODIAC PARADE: A Celestial Journey Through the Stars
Text Copyright © 2026 Ashley Johnson
Illustrations Copyright © Indira Audiprathana
Paperback ISBN 978-1-962140-55-3
Hardcover ISBN 978-1-962140-51-5

To schedule author events or order in bulk, visit the Books & Things Publishing website at www.booksandthingspublishing.com

For the little stargazers
who whisper secrets to the
moon, count constellations
past bedtime, and believe
the sky is listening. May
you always know the stars
above and the magic within
are guiding you.

Come one, come all, from near and far,
To see a parade with every star!
Twelve little signs up in the sky,
Each with a twinkle and reason why!

Aries is the first to cheer,
A brave young ram with no hint of fear.
Charging forward, bold and bright,
A fireball full of morning light.

Taurus loves to rest and eat,
A gentle bull with steady feet.
Loves soft blankets, books, and cake,
And naps beneath a quiet lake.

Gemini can talk all day,
The twins will chat and laugh and play.
Quick and clever, always new,
With stories, jokes, and riddles too!

Cancer wears a cozy shell,
The crab who cares and hugs so well.
Loves the moon and home so dear,
Protecting all who venture near.

Leo roars with lion pride,
So full of joy it cannot hide!
A golden heart, a starry crown,
The king or queen of every town!

Virgo keeps things neat and clean,
The wisest one you've ever seen.
They love to help and plan ahead,
With books and lists beside their bed.

Libra balances left and right,
A scale that seeks what's fair and right.
With beauty, peace, and grace so grand,
They bring calm to all the land.

Scorpio is strong and sly,
With secrets shining in each eye.
They feel so deep, they know what's true,
A loyal friend through and through.

Sagittarius rides a starry horse,
Adventure is their favorite course!
With bow and arrow aimed so high,
They chase their dreams across the sky.

Capricorn climbs every hill,
A mountain goat with iron will.
They work so hard and reach the top,
Step by step, they never stop.

Aquarius is full of spark;
A thinker glowing in the dark.
Ideas fly like bubbles in the sea,
They dream of peace throughout the galaxy.

Pisces swims in waters deep,
Where magic flows and daydreams sleep.
With art and song, they float along,
And turn the world into a song.

Twelve bright signs in skies so wide,
Each with their twinkle, side by side.
A parade of stars, a cosmic gleam,
The zodiac signs form one great team.

9 781962 140553